Slowly, As If

KAREN PRESS lives in Cape Town. She has published eight poetry collections as well as mathematics textbooks and children's books. Her poetry has appeared in journals in South Africa, Britain, the United States, Australia and Canada, and in translation in French, Italian, Turkish and Tamil. She co-founded the publishing collective Buchu Books and currently works as a freelance editor and writer.

KAREN PRESS

Slowly, As If

CARCANET

Earlier versions of some of the poems in this book have appeared in
*New Coin, Green Dragon, Chimurenga, The African Cities Reader, Counter-Currents
Pagine* and *Anglistica.*

First published in Great Britain in 2012 by

Carcanet Press Limited
Alliance House
Cross Street
Manchester M2 7AQ

www.carcanet.co.uk

A CIP catalogue record for this book is available from the British Library

ISBN 978 1 84777 136 0

The publisher acknowledges financial assistance from Arts Council England

Typeset by XL Publishing Services, Tiverton
Printed and bound in England by SRP Ltd, Exeter

Contents

'PHOTOGRAPHING THE BUILDING IS FORBIDDEN UNTIL THE WAR IS OVER'

1

A relief supply ship for the bombed citizens of Iraq
called *Sir Galahad*
arrives tomorrow in the port of Basra.

Oh where is the beautiful lady
who will come out of the charred crowd
to lay her long hair along the shore
and wave the green scarf of welcome?

How they dream themselves good,
the madmen of the West.

2

The poets gird their loins again.
Outrage. Metaphors. The assonance of keening.
There are enough poems lamenting war to last for eternity.

All we can offer are images of horror in modern dress,
all we can do is confirm that helplessness includes
life in a fine apartment overlooking cityscapes,
spin doctors, cell phones and cappuccinos
for the unexpectedly last time before the glass shatters
and the eyes are burnt beyond recognition.

Forgive us, people digging through your bombed houses
with wails as raw as each buried limb you glimpse,
forgive us for finding metaphors inside your torn shirts and
                                                bleeding dogs.

Forgive us, captured American soldier, if we hear you
tell your captors 'I come to fix broke stuff'
and find in your half-formed logic
the voice of a machine still being tested for defects.

Our words mean everything we've learned about them
and it is right that we don't have words for the feeling of
                                        being destroyed,
there should be no words for destruction,
it is the moment for silence
in every language in the world.

3

Raindrops stay on the leaves a long time.
The birds sip at them without breaking the sparkling nets.

The ground around every landmine holds its breath
for the moment when fire will explode its seeds into life.

Nature made everything, even the B-52 and George Bush.
Patterns of screaming children travel far into international airspace

melting the ice on every jet's wings,
sending it in to land ahead of schedule.

4

In their different ways

a war-torn country
a war-torn province
a war-torn region
a war-torn community
a war-torn house
a war-torn friendship
a war-torn memory
a war-torn body
a war-torn poem
a war-torn understanding
a war-torn room
a war-torn tree

5

(Margin note:
something not mentioned in the reports
or seen in the photographs whose captions
misdirect your attention –

the child's wounded body is always shaded by a man
crouching there with desperate eyes,
waving away insects or touching the bandages
as if there were something he could do
to mend the exploded flesh

and at funerals there are so many men
crying over the little body

even if they have locked their women inside houses and
                                        windowless clothing,
even if they carry guns and wear beards,
even if their turbans contain great hatred,
these men would give their lives to save this small child,
these men with broken hearts.)

6

Walking between George Bush and a full heart
I choose the path of trees and cobbles
in a familiar city full of foreigners.

To be invisible in a place you know well
is the best kind of freedom.
There's so much chatter in the world,
only silence now would change anything.
George Bush shadows me as I walk, complete
power and powerlessness on a street where trees do what the
                                        wind wants
and cobbles grow slowly softer in profile,
footstep by footstep.

Whether or not I love you you'll sleep well tonight.
In my heart too you'll sleep well, close to me.
I'll breathe in time to the wind.
George Bush passing through these hours
will leave only the lightest footprints.

7

On the record
the bombs kept falling
long after the journalists had left.

Off the record
he went out when he could
in the early morning hours
to watch the sky change colour undisturbed
and his wife sometimes joined him.

Once a reporter saw them walking, holding hands,
and he felt he should run after her
to explain.

8

Will the war be over
when people are dying of hunger instead of bomb strikes?
When the victors run out of new weapons to test?
When their radioactive debris has finished decaying on
                                        the battlefields?
When the sad little wingless men they bred in captivity
climb up on the podium
and announce that they are the leaders
of the new democracy?

The barbed wire around the US consulate
will come down when the war is over.
We can stop praying and chanting outside the
                        unphotographable building,

4

holding these placards that blow so wildly in the southeaster
we nearly get knocked down
when the war is over.

The oil price will stabilise when the war is over.
Holiday travel will be safe again when the war is over.
Everyone will be happy when the war is over,
and we can take photographs of ourselves smiling.

Your Saddam

A man emerges
from a hole in the ground
wild-eyed, shaggy,

lost among lenses and muzzles
that drive him into the hands
of white-coated men

whose gloved fingers
prise open his jaw,
probe the soft flesh inside his mouth,

tilt his chin away from his neck,
expose his pitted skin to the light
push his swollen tongue aside,

scrape evidence out of him and display it –
surely calling up pity and horror
in all who see him this way.
If you saw him this way
you'd surely push through the bellowing soldiers, the
                                        ravening journalists
to lead him to safety, you'd reach out to touch him,

smooth the rough hair from his face,
capture his confused hands
and fill them with this warmth that wells up in your chest

until it wants to burst, this same hot ache you feel
when you see any wounded living thing.
What must you do with this human self

that ambushes you with its eagerly spilling sympathy,
splashing it into the torn hands of a man,
of this particular man?

Who is betrayed in this no-man's-land
where your heart unfolds its wings
like a child playing at being an angel

and is caught in the spotlight
of his victims' eyes,
every one of them staring at you?

CYRUS VANCE SAT ON MY COUCH

Cyrus Vance sat on my couch,
the curved pale blue one with the coffee stain
that Saul and David left behind in the Scott Road house.
I should have kept that couch.
Saul's a famous historian now
and David's an even more famous medical scientist.
I have a smaller second-hand couch these days,
covered in white bull denim, it cost R20
from Barkhoff's up the road from that house
and it's served me well, but Cyrus Vance wouldn't have
                                        fitted on it.

He was a big man in a suit, of course,
and there must have been other big men with him
that day but I can't remember where they all fitted
in my semi-detached lounge, perhaps they stood behind the couch.
Who was he meeting there,
apart from my obvious friend,
and did we have coffee and biscuits
(the way the security police brought their own
custard slices with them when they arrived
to interrogate Welma in her flat)?

I was one of the crowd back then
as now, he wouldn't even have seen I was in the room,
in a corner, staring at my couch with him on it.
Even though it was my house.

What did he think of that scruffy street and the living room,
mould up the walls and Venda cloths covering the chairs?
A house built for nineteenth-century families who seldom ate meat
                                        or bathed.
And that strange trailing fern we had on the mantelpiece
                        with its fat bundles of fronds
that lived another fifteen years after I left the house –
did its spores make him sneeze?

Later that year I had dinner at a long yellowwood table
                                at Rozenhof Restaurant
where Robert McNamara held forth,
apparently here on some kind of peace mission
and all the recipients of Ford money sat dutifully around the
                                table looking at our plates,
thinking of napalm and Vietnamese palm trees
and children falling through his fingers
like the breadcrumbs falling away from our knives.

These men were like visitors from outer space
to us, but in fact we were their outer space,
aliens they were trying to steer into their holding pens.
They didn't even get indigestion.
They didn't even get dust on their shoes.
They talked and talked and talked even when they were listening
and here we all are twenty years later,
just as they planned it.

THE DAISY CUTTER

The Daisy Cutter is a bomb
designed to incinerate everything
animal, vegetable and mineral
within a 600-metre radius.

It creates a giant blast wave
that flattens the landscape
around the point of impact.

Hence the name 'daisy cutter'.

It's the most powerful weapon
in the American arsenal
except for nuclear bombs.

The US Army is testing it now
on the people and daisies of Afghanistan.

A COW AND A GOOSE

A cow and a goose came to my door one day.

'We don't want to die,' they said with one voice.

There are so many different ways to respond to two
                              strange animals
who come to your door and say something like that.
For example, 'Why not?' and 'We all have to die.'
or, 'What do you expect me to do about that?'
or, 'Why are you here?'
but especially, 'Where did you learn to speak English?'

I felt too confused to say anything at all.
To my shame I put out a saucer of milk
and went back to my novel.

The next day they came back.
'I'm sorry,' I said this time. 'The milk was stupid.'
Then I was stuck.

They wandered around my garden for a bit,
to give me time to come up with something more useful.
When they got back to where I was standing they said again,
slightly more slowly, 'We really don't want to die.'

'Nor do I,' I said.
It was the only true thing that came to mind.

SPECIALISED

'Ammunition Airlift During the Relief of Khe Sanh,
South Vietnam, April, 1968'

photograph by Larry Burrows

The helicopter – it has the strangest shape,
a big head bending low, a long thin body,
dangling wheel-legs, like a dachshund
with a shortened snout – is lowering
a crate the size of its head on chains
towards the green ribbing of a terraced hill,
as bare-chested men smeared with grease
prepare to grab hold of the descending weight.

How does the ammunition in the crate
not explode on impact with the hill?
Or in transit, jostling against the tarpaulin, the slats,
the crosswinds on this cloudy Vietnamese day?

There must have been a whole research project
devoted to making just this one moment possible:
transport techniques for volatile explosive *matériel*,
over so many miles moving from that altitude to this,
in these and other weather conditions,
in these and other degrees of humidity,
for immediate or later detonation
at this latitude, among these hills.

It must have started many years ago
when someone imagined that this
would be necessary one day.

A budget, a search for laboratory staff,
an explosives chemist headhunted,
simulation chambers designed,
raw materials extracted
from the blind earth.

How long did it take,
this one element of mastery,
to evolve?

Homo sapiens. Homo sapiens sapiens.

Skypointing

Skypointing in appeasement
is what gannets do

as they step carefully through
their crowded coastal colonies

exposing longly vulnerable necks
to the massed brothersister citizens

and keeping beaks shut tight
raised high above temptations of the flesh

that make their eyes gleam:
a bit of spare space or a dead fish

glimpsed in a secret squint
below the horizon of safe gazing

not allowed not allowed
to take to take

walk on walk on good gannet
looking skyward signifies the humble self

its mind on other things Up There
blue things invisible Higher Things

take nothing take nothing good gannet
good skypointing gannet.

~

Humans skypoint
to signal war

thrusting throats thick with cursing prayers
across the air blasting warning displays

strutting heavily forward flinging arms wide
across cities seas deserts forests feathers fins fur flesh

preparing to vaporise all things bright and beautiful,
eyes offered to the blinding sun

they call their own
God's light

call it down unblinkingly to kill
all in a good cause good cause invisible sky cause

blank eyes upturned let their lips touch
everything they smell lick the salt from the blood

moving further into it
skypointing God's good guns.

AND ALL THE TIME

Venice, 11 September 2001

Venice came to fetch me at the station.

I was on my way from Tremosine to Refrontolo
via Santa Lucia, just a coffee
and a glimpse of platform life would have made me happy
but Venice came to fetch me
and said stay a few hours,
here's the Canale Grande to keep you safe
from melancholy, come,
walk down the steps,
even the American teenagers are doing it,
it's easy.

It was really Venice,
the whole movie set
smiling at me, hands outstretched.

Marco Polo. Serge Diaghilev. Joseph Brodsky. Me.

The movie where you fall in love
with the stranger in the piazza
and he looks back at you as he walks away
and his eyes say follow me ...
and you become the woman
he wants to be followed by,
and the gondola waits for you
in the small canal framed by lamplit palace windows.

~

At this distance,
             at this remove,
   I recall stormy weather – the sunlit patches of it –

the grey dockside where hard-eyed young Hassidim
                           were drinking tea,
and the closed faces of the walls around Campo del Ghetto –

the storm reaching me as I got there,
shepherding me back along Rio Terra San Leonardo,
across the Canale di Cannaregio and through Lista di Spagna,
        with its blazing clouds and black showers
    showing me where to hurry

as I elbowed among the crowds
    and crowds of young Americans on every bridge,
                    at every intersection –

the sky's gold angel wings beating
over empty houses
                melting into rain behind me,
its thunderous murmur urging me toward shelter
as the light grew deeper,
hurrying across bridges past
                    the dusk-pink waters of secret kisses,
        flashes of blonde piazzas where little churches
                        hummed to themselves,
    men studied windows filled with costumes for
                            a masked ball,
        a dog dozed against a barrow of maps,
    two women compared aubergines against the light,

into a cathedral where young boys sent the silver shafts
                            of their voices
into the dark
        and an old lady knelt alone,
to wait

until the rain stopped, it was safe to run for the station,

to sit near three Romany men making an espresso last
            the long damp hour before a train came
to take them somewhere else, or leave them behind

and the Americans buzzing and bartering at every corner
called each other to look at the pillars, the walls,

the barges with their singing cargo,
        sent each other promises and addresses
across the choppy canals shining in the mottled stormlight
to meet later, to meet tomorrow.

        ~

The sky cleared, there was time before nightfall
to step away
            onto an island of death, blindingly white
            and tidy, its graves and gravestones
            rigid as lacquered hair,
            its grass in uniform, its wreaths marking time
            in plastic and satin melodic precision –

only the miniature toys, the tractor the truck and the dinosaur
on a little boy's grave toppled this way and that
in the wind, too light to lie still.

At this distance I wonder
where they were in the hour after I left,
the young Americans, when the message came,
and silence fell over them,
and they started to flee –

        ~

Venice let me leave without prophecies or warnings,
handing me back my eyes and tickets onward with an easy smile
and as I tried to scatter coins of thanks in my wake
waved them aside
                    saying only,
            you're welcome here, it's no trouble
            to hold all of this open to you, it weighs nothing,
            you weigh nothing,

like mist you pass over my skin
and I am not here, this city is emptiness

in the shape of a dream, a dream's shell,
an old shell rolling in waters no one can enter.

~

And all the time the world was changing
and there was no sign of it,
no turbulence in the canals,
no sudden scattering of the birds and men.

My 9/11 was a day in a city
with nothing better to do than cloak me lightly
in a thundercloud of antique beauty,
like all the future's ghosts
I was free to wander here, watching heaven's storms gather
and spill
and the small gold flares that catch the cobblestones
afterwards in the wet silence where clouds soften
and sunlight drips down its walls.

Monument to the South African Republic

(on some photographs by David Goldblatt)

The long dry grass collects our history
and every few years burns it off
in a frenzy of memory.

Here it grows for two policemen who died
for the same cause, in Afrikaans and Zulu,
and who lie in heartfelt English
among broken cans and paper scraps
the grass has gathered for them,
for my lovely husband, from his lovely wife and children.

And here, around a modest stone obelisk,
memorial to the dead republic
erected on the day of its birth, the grass sways its long stalks
dried to the colour of biblical corn, sifting the summer wind
that brings grains of brick, cement,
old seeds and dog hairs to form a carpet
for the sparrows that visit, the tramps who sleep here –
for the town has understood to build
its street of chain stores and municipal offices
leading in the other direction, away from this
weathered, semi-literate scrap of older time.

In a graveyard a white concrete arch
loses its letters one by one leaving their grey shadows
behind like stains, vow of the dead soldiers
who came to rest here in a flag-shaped myth,
and the grass leaves a bare gravel patch
naked to the sun lest we forget, lest we forget
how nothing grows from such valour.

But just beyond the borderline of thirsty eucalyptus trees
it grows again, long and soft and ready to catch
someone's cigarette, some beer bottle splinter
smouldering there after a raucous night of farewells
and burn fast, and lay itself down as ash over the past.

Ravenous

The baby white-eyes watch their parents
aim for the fattest figs
and rip their red hearts out,
chirping with rampant morning joy.

They're lime yellow and green banana green,
small as cake forks and just as single-minded.

Eviscerated figs dangle like traitors
from the old grey branches
as the predators move on,
swoop on the guava tree's fans of fresh leaves.
Each guava gives up its softness
to the scimitar beaks without flinching,
its yellow skin
splayed in a ragged halo.

Now the purple grapes beckon,
and the bursting apricots:
this is summer,
a time for devouring sweetness.

EIGHT FRESCOES FROM THE LOST PALACES OF ZANJ

the furious women bare themselves

the furious women bare themselves
issuing a challenge no man should accept

to the troops invading the squatter camp
in buffels and ratels spiked with guns

smoke races from cooking fires and burning houses
the armoured vehicles have shuttered their windows

dare to look, dare to look
the naked women shout at the helmeted boys

who close their eyes as they advance
in the driving rain, rifles cocked and dripping

charcoal streaks erase the sky
iron walls buckle and the women's bodies shine like sweat,
                                                    like steel

rain soaks the soldiers' shirts
the women feel the ash stroking their thighs, their bellies

smoke puffs erupt like kisses from the guns

the four students run for the border

the four students run for the border
with ochre footsteps remembering their land

from all sides blond hair thorns and blue spear thorns
                                        pierce their skin
and fear summons its shadows to track them

but they keep running bright-eyed,
thirsty as buck for the green clearing that must lie ahead

to the left the earth is cracking
tyre tracks slither forward hungrily

to the right mottled commandos leopard-crawl over the
                                        soft new growth
crushing the water out of its skin

the four friends are almost at the end
their fingertips reach for the barbed wire fence

they are leaping,
all their bright blood is leaping

he hides all night while they murder his family

he hides all night while they murder his family

the shadow of a cold street
and the shadow of his body hunched like a fist in one corner

light of a window,
shadows moving like cries behind glass

how much you can hear when it's so dark

the lord is my shepherd I shall not want
my lamb is called Boo
what colour is that?
yellow!

such bright clear yellow
flame bright

the shadow of his body
is beating like a heart

like a shot, and another, and another

he holds himself
there is nothing but darkness here
his breath carries him through it like wind

no one can stop the wind, he lets himself go with it

they were caught and chained in a van

they were caught and chained in a van

they look lovingly out over the veld
as the van drives, drives and drives

laughter and memory pour from their eyes
through the bars, streaking the air with sunset oranges and pinks

as the van drives through the bitter winter fields
swerving and braking, slamming their bodies against metal walls

a boy who taught hens to circle dance
a girl who cut bibles into true stories

this is their last journey and they are escaping
breath by breath onto the road, through the dry grass

towards the fields where the cosmos flowers every year
despite the drought, magenta and mauve armies, self-seeding

goodbye, they are calling to each telegraph pole,
goodbye, goodbye

she gave birth while prison guards tortured her and laughed

she gave birth while prison guards tortured her and laughed

only a goddess could do this,
and now without the sun's blazing chariot
or a cloak of thunder,
without spirits or eagles or rivers to command

she must be a goddess alone,
must leave her human heart somewhere helpless
and roar until she broke open

in a grey cell, bearing a daughter who would hate her
for the smell of laughing vultures that entered her at birth
and never left her

only a goddess could survive this
with clear eyes and a graceful back
sweeping the yard of her freedom without regret
unloved and magnificent

a six-year-old boy is digging a grave for a baby

a six-year-old boy is digging a grave for a baby

he finds a red marble
and a strange metal thing like a buckle, with sharp points

he watches an ant drag a crumb of apple flesh towards the grave
and digs a shallow trench to steer the ant in a safe direction

when the hole is as deep as his knees
he starts to make footholds in the walls
like a mountaineer's ascent path

russet leaves keep blowing into the grave
he presses them into the tops of the walls, a frieze

he makes a small cave in one wall, a storage chamber
for the marble, the buckle, and the other apple someone gave him

then he fetches the baby in its shroud,
places it in the grave and curls up next to it

he watches the ants as they make a path around the baby
taking crumbs of earth and leaves to the corner

where they're digging a tunnel

the colours there

the colours there

brown hands
white stones

green wind tumbling through green grass
blue water blue sky
and the grey veils of winter

tangled together across so many years
rope of cold longing

a prison rainbow

like paper flowers unfolding in water

like paper flowers unfolding in water

the artists swirl through halls and corridors,
releasing the shapes no one has named yet

of things once remembered and often dreamed

their arcs and spirals unleash every story
dissolving it in the unlocked light

of these crumbled palaces
gone ahead of the historian's pencil

vanishing into the archives of passing raindrops

until only pale shadows are left
that spill onto fingertips touching the stones

a faint sparkle

that could be dust of ancient seeds, or gold, or words

Local fauna

One of the strange creatures you find in this country
is me
small and almost invisible,
sending mixed signals
or no signals
depending on the weather and the time of day.

I've been called many things
I don't answer to.

Mispronounced in one of two ways
I accept responsibility for your desire to have me
lift my head and look familiar.

For the rest,
I'm doing what I'm doing
in a story you haven't read.

I grow well here
except for certain seasons that come every few days
when I need to be somewhere else,
in another plotline,
unscrewing the stars from their perches, or
skateboarding over neat women and their pavements.

I eat what comes,
taste of sea water laced with tar,
have no distinctive call or coloration.

In your guide books
I'd be the space at the bottom of a page
made for your notes, your reminders and discoveries.

BE BEAR

Be bear, the doctor says, be crane
and tiger and golden pheasant, be monkey and dragon.

Fold in and open, gather and strike,
wake the dragon and tame the tiger,
catch the monkey, balance where the crane does
all day and all night, open-winged on one leg

and attack, when necessary attack
or soften and fall, become a dragon
becoming a folding pheasant.

NON SEQUITUR

These two men count the unemployed
by race
by gender
by age
by province
by education
by sector

in Greek letters
and Roman numerals
and American funding
they count them
with eighteen tables
and fourteen figures
and three appendices –

those they've found
in ten years of raw data –

and there are fewer, but more
and they have moved, but they're still there,
and they grow older, but their youth multiplies

and the only adjective that visits them is
(for a certain segment of a graph)
discouraged –

a particular category of workseeker
with a quite specific meaning

but in the last line of their book these two men say,
as if they'd just walked out of someone's leaning shack,
as if they'd just watched seven children fighting over
                                    one small nectarine,

'someone must do something
for the unemployed, whose lives are terrible'

and so we know that even counting work
starts because there are men who feel
the misery of other men

and end their days with ragged eyes
staring at silent spreadsheets wishing
they could turn them into a thousand loaves and fishes,
a hundred, one –
just one.

IN THE EMPTY STATION

'Birds fly through the empty station,' says Tom,
and I think of Gare du Nord and that Turkish family
who all wore black cashmere coats and hats
and carried hot drinks in paper cups away from the kiosk,
with nowhere to sit they huddled against each other,
it was freezing, the wind was blowing a November night
into the terminus hall, you'd insisted on coming
even though you hate France and I didn't ask you to,
you just made your own plans to join me
which clearly didn't obey you
because there I was pacing up and down
the charcoal platform hour after hour,
there were pigeons fluttering high above the lines,
shadowy shapes scraping the grey glass roof,
the rusted buffers were the warmest colour there.
Why did you come, you spent the whole week
on the phone to someone else
in the tiny nest I'd settled into,
there wasn't really space for you anyway
and you were late, your train got stuck
somewhere on a border, the station seemed empty
even though streams of people were moving through
including eventually you striding towards me
furious with the concept of national boundaries
and we went out into the city where you don't live,
I knew the way by now,
and in the empty station birds continued to fly.

Man series I

Man holding a puppy.

Man stumbling back and forth
across the traffic lanes, spittle trailing
from the corners of his mouth.

Man making omelettes at a deserted hotel
for two foreign women who work while they eat,
small fluffy omelettes to eat in the warm rain on the terrace.

Man getting out of bed to fetch an extra blanket
for the woman asleep next to him,
in case the winter air wakes her.

Man carrying a woman's cases through the rain
at midnight, from an airport terminal into a car,
swift and silent.

Man, behind previous man,
forcing himself forward with an umbrella
and a hand demanding a dollar.

Man in vagrant clothes
facing a woman's determined camera.

Man carrying a crying boy into a field.

Man following two women up a road
treading on their heels, and when they say
'Please leave us alone'
crossing to the other side of the road
and keeping step with them, grinning.

Man, snow-covered, arriving at the door
with a stack of birch logs in his arms
to feed his dying friend's stove.

Man overtaking on a blind rise
then forcing his way back into the queue
one car ahead.

Man clipping his toenails
in a first class carriage of the Frankfurt-Paris InterCity Express.

Man laying his head on an older man's shoulder
while they watch the Senegal-Cameroon match
from the older man's sickbed.

Man walking naked into a room
where someone lies sleeping.

Six Eggs in the Fridge

Six eggs in the fridge.
Six eggs on the table.

They say you should eat eggs
from time to time.

Six eggs in the fridge.
That was the April resolution.

Six eggs on the table.
That's this week's resolution.

January's eggs went down the drain
in six small sticky glugs,
shrunken old men eggs.

Every few months I get a yearning
for soft scrambled eggs with salmon and dill
for a five pm breakfast

and that's when I realise how easy it is to cook eggs.
They say you should eat eggs
from time to time.

Beautiful shit-speckled brown organic grain-fed eggs –
for sure their mothers spend their days pecking at daisies
in the grass around a barn door,
within clucking distance of a fresh basket.

So these eggloads of unhatched energy wait
in the fridge
on the table

cool spirals of DNA
embalmed miracles
embryonic generations

while I have the smell of chocolate on my fingers
and jars of lentils turning to dust in my cupboard
and earfuls of free advice about eggs.

MINDFULNESS

In a sunlit circle of silence I sit
like a midday flower that breathes in heat,
breathes out fragrance.

This silence.
This breath.
My quiet universe.

Around the edges a million people
cheerfully hold out the things I'll need
any minute now:

water,
a sandwich,
medicine,
toilet paper,
my jacket,
a light bulb.

Fluttering shadows like the outer petals of my flower.

Making my peace
with their busy clatter
all over the world

dare I ask them to work
more quietly?

Dare I train my mind
to empty itself of them?

THANK YOU LEE SMOLIN, THANK YOU MR LEIBNIZ

So we're monads after all,
that's a relief, complete and separate
and also connected to every other agglomeration of
                                    fundamental particles
(aka pine cone, parking meter, vodka orange)
we've ever touched however tangentially,
boson from a breath of Plato's used air
gone two millennia later into the feather of
                                    a chicken in Mumbai,
air I exhale full of fermions from the fourth king of
                                    Axum's coronation dinner,
so that if you read any electron's palm now you can tell
what it will be feeling in 4005.

All this proven by science.

I love science, it radiates more imagination and longing
than all the love poems ever published
and it makes me understand why I'd rather be alone
recollecting the touch of a dog's paws on my shoulders
(his paws and my shoulders changed forever)
than listening to ten of my fellow citizens
talking about what's wrong with the state of the roads
in a country with no work ethic
and not enough ubuntu –

these roads peopled with whispers of Einstein's pipe smoke,
each gently describing everything else
without making a fuss about it,
and with no illusion that the world revolves
around what it has to say,

even though it does,
as science is increasingly showing us to be true.

IF YOU WROTE ABOUT DOMESTIC THINGS

If you wrote about domestic things
you'd never go wrong.

Even the emperor of the world has to scrub his nails
worrying at the flake of skin that won't come loose.

In every kitchen there are stains that no one knows
                                        how to get rid of,
embarrassing uncertainties on sheets, dish towels
                                        needing help,

and the poignancy of a crumb of bread
that never diminishes, the whole history of soldiers
                            and children shines there.

Once we did get out of the car

Once we did get out of the car:
dry grass at ankle height, brown and grey stones
with sharp edges softened by surface dust.
Bleached brown ground as hard as cement.

Look, a black beetle. A grey gecko.
Look, is it a snake?
No, barbed wire from a broken fence.
Watch out for spikes.
Watch out for thorns.
What's that over there?
A bird.

We got back in the car:
pass me a hardboiled egg, pass the salt.
There are apples at the back;
let's go.

Outside the left window:
a sunset spilling pink and orange syrup over purple mountains.
Outside the right window:
a full moon rising like a giant pearl.
Look. Look.

Men always have an idea

Men always have an idea
about going off somewhere

on their own,
someone to see, something to do,

nothing you need to know about.

They'll be back in their own time,
they'll kiss the rope that tethers them to you

and then go off again.
They like to play in different places.

To leave without explaining anything
and come back without explaining anything,

that's what makes life good.

Women need to know where you were
every hour of the day, and what you did, and with whom,

and how often you thought of them
before they can love you.

SHINE

Being told
you're made of stardust
is not helpful
as you sit holding a parking ticket
(is it also made of stardust)
and the copy of the registered letter of appeal
you wrote a month ago

while the City Police call centre
(stardust, all of it)
flies you through optical fibre space
from one logging-appeals terminal to another
in search of a verdict.

You are stardust that parked in a loading zone,
that's the verdict.

Pay the damned fine, justice isn't a chemical element
anywhere in the known universe.

Then you can go out and shine
the way you were designed to do.

THE SAD LITTLE POEMS

I like the sad little poems that poets write to themselves
when they're sitting at windows on hot nights
unable to write
anything worth calling a poem.
They're like drinks you buy yourself
in a bar on a rainy night when you're feeling homeless
                                    and sub-human,
you look at the guy next to you and know
he's also going to have the hardest time
getting through the night,
not even a dog would walk home with him,
you buy him a drink as well
and neither of you starts a conversation.

Sad little poems with no dog to walk home.
And I thank the editors
who leave them in the collections,
even though they have nothing to say
to the readers out there
who want something more fragrant,
with a recognisable main character.

PASTERNAK'S SHADOW

The chapter recounts how Stalin phoned Pasternak
to ask who Mandelstam was, if he was a 'master' –
and explains what Pasternak surely knew at once,
that Stalin was asking whether and what he would lose
if he followed his first instinct: to kill the poet.
Yes, Pasternak told him, Mandelstam is a master,
and saved the poet's life
for the endlessness of an exile
and the whisper of a prison death.

What made Stalin feel threatened
by this small man's unwritten poem?
the chapter goes on to ask and struggles to answer,
but I've stayed behind
in the room where Pasternak looks at the telephone,
I can see how his hand is shaking
as he breathes in what he's just done.

Of course Mandelstam is a master
and if he, Pasternak, with one clear syllable uttered in a daze
has saved the poet's life for the time it takes
a small boy to swoop past him on his toboggan,
his red face brighter than the sun of this unending winter,
he can live with himself another day
inside Stalin's cold protective shadow.

But the question that rises up
like the shadow of that shadow
will not leave him now,
it clings to his soul like a forest leech:
if it had been another poet,
if it had been the man three streets away
who shows him his dull rhymes about birches and soldiers
or the woman whose love poems
have been clogging his letter box for years,
if it had been the professor who writes stale odes
in praise of nothing living,

would he have called each one 'master'
for the sake of their lives?

Would he stand up inside the mask of his freedom
and burn his own fine-tuned tongue
to keep one of them warm?
He wants to tear the telephone loose from its wall
so that there can be no more –
but he dare not – what if Stalin has Akhmatova's name
scrawled on a pad in front of him,
with a question mark?

Love songs for Lake Como

1

The lake is learning blueness from the sky.
It's spring: trees at its edges urge it on,
already far into their green thirst.

Slowly the water lightens but there's black below,
and a silver shadow folding each bright ripple in —
the deepness and the memory of the lake

it clings to, for the sky is far away
and blue without conversation. The trees say nothing,
blue is their dream of sweet fruit

but in the end it is the lake's life at stake here,
its loneliness and its future.

2

The clouds and the mist and the snow
won't let go of this silver place
as spring comes with its green paintbox,
its almond brushstrokes up and down the black branches.

Through every cleft they can find in the hills
the clouds wind their wistful scarves.
Shawls of mist drift to the water's edge
leaving their taste on the cypresses,
swallowing the boat engine's heat
before it can warm the lake's skin.

High on the peaks snow stitches its last lace to the stone
like an exiled woman climbing, turning back
to throw her memories over the lost land

as if they could freeze there and wait for her,
turning to crystals, turning to lake light.

Val di Bondo

White stones in river water.
Silver bark flakes.
Green flesh of unripe hazelnuts.
Purple geraniums.
Orange pumpkins.

This is where light comes from
in a valley between northern mountains.

Amsterdam night

Throwing my ticket into the canal
was a way to meet the cold red air
of that doorstep where we sat, drinking
the hours until the snow arrived.

All night I walked corner to corner with you
looking for the right moment. Once we were stabbed
trying to seize it, then we knew we should settle
for the quiet glow of that room where a barman watched
and a woman in a pink sweater held a tiny brass spoon
to her face, sprinkling a story of lost love over us.

OVER THERE

Berlin, November 1989

Once I was in a city that held me back
until the last moment

so I walked its autumn hours, waiting,
walked a small trail through streets
with their faces turned to the wall,
their memories packed for flight,
their passports withering

but the city said, sit here, wait with me,
it can't be much longer,
something is brewing, hatching, ticking,
it can't go on like this, I can't

~

The underground is at the end of its years
in the east,
in the west, too.

The red velvet *kaffeehaus* chairs are worn through,
the patrons are worn down with coffee and cigarettes
and the children they had when already somewhat mature,
slumped over wrinkled copies of *taz* at the pre-war
                              wooden tables,
drinking their bowls of milky chocolate and thimbles of espresso
while their little anarchist heirs wail and wander around,
throwing fragments of television nursery rhymes at strangers
as if hoping for some entertainment in return,
something new from the invisible wonderland
da drüben, they're confused
about where it is, the one they belong to.

At this time the patrons correctly have nothing to say
to the packs of journalists stalking the quarter
where yesterday's enemies face off
through the blank stares of their young men
held on the leash in the police vans idling in side streets:
the bullets are still real, still as real as the blood,
that's what keeps everyone strung tight like violin wire
on a treasured instrument that just won't sing,
as if the air's too hard or the sky too bare.

The patrons have earned their clairvoyance
with years and years of graffiti and underground news
and the hunger of those who stay loyal to the old forests
while new agro-economies are flourishing
on the faraway steppes and the prairies.

They can tell you how it will end for them, for you,
on the other side and the other other side,
they won't be the first to run laughing across the border
the wrong way, making it disappear with their own bodies,
they don't really want to see the other half
of the city that will blame them for being here and for
                                                    not being
more shiny than this, for not being New York or Frankfurt
or anywhere in California.

And there, on that side,
the underground has ground to a halt just before the border,
the last roll of tickets hangs limply from the machine,
the platforms stand still, as bare as an empty sanatorium
when all the patients have been released
healthy again, ready to fill the streets with their happy
                                                    intentions.

Only one soldier patrols slowly
up and down, up and down,
letting the sound of his boots on the bare cement
hypnotise him for the last time
in this quiet grey dream
they've already started chipping at just two blocks away:

the full city is coming to fetch the empty city,
from both sides the noise is growing,
the cars, the hands reaching out,
the welcome money and the bananas,
and the children wailing in the old red *kaffeehaus*.

History wants to
get its hands on this city
all over again.

~

The great thing about a wall
is that it means what it says.

So when it comes down
there's no doubt about it:
something phenomenological is different,
something material has changed.

And the great thing about a balloon
being wound and knotted into the long pink shape
of a dachshund at ten to nine on a Thursday night
in a cabaret circus club full of smoke and wine
is that it proves how serious grown-ups are about playing.

So that when someone stops
winding an orange balloon into the shape of a rabbit
and cries out listen to the radio! the wall is down!
you know this is completely serious
and could only happen in a cabaret
about history in a city with no country to keep it warm.

And the great thing about Potsdamer Strasse
in November 1989 is how cold it was,
poor-migrants-selling-their-old-clothes-cold,
Baltic-Caspian-Black-Sea-Siberian-wind-cold
up and down the wide barren pavements,
and the thrift shops offering black flannel nightshirts
worn thin but with their rich colour unfaded,

black polo necks of the thinnest nylon,
black trilbies for small-headed men,
fifty pfennig each, cheap warmth for a solitary foreigner
waiting for the city to say, it's over, you can go now.

So that sitting in a café with a bowl of hot chocolate
held in both hands seemed like the warmest softest
                                        place on earth
and the black clothes shone against the grey cement of winter
like a forest still intact.

And walking in a slow million-person circle
around the wall with its tiny perforations,
its teenagers with their fathers' hammers straddling the top,
its helmet-headed men sheltering their machine guns
from the crowd, the laughing million-person *Wesi* crowd
draped with the shawls of television lights
leaning in closer and closer to feel
the heartbeat of history changing its rhythm

you could imagine how cold it was on the other side,
and reach across, and blow clouds of your warm Western breath
right onto the walls of the old monuments.

                ~

I stayed through that first weekend
when the city swelled and burst,
festering with desire and joy.

The underground trains burned out,
the first *Osi* fists were raised against the Turkish
                                    migrants in the West,
the KaDeWe refused to donate its thousand brands of butter
or its in-store lavatories
to the wide-eyed brothers and sisters discovering
the nature of capitalist consumption,
its riches and its punishments.

By the next Monday everyone was sitting staring at the ground,
wondering where they lived now,
and who it belonged to

and I left, carrying a walled city in my left eye
and an unwalled city in my right,
my own before-and-after synapses of history

up Oranienburgstrasse, back through Schöneberg,
across the bare patch of rubble where they filmed
                              Wings of Desire,
my black-and-white city with its orange rabbit balloon
never to be knotted by the young magician
fading behind me,

each of us pulling our old overcoats tighter,
walking in thin shoes our separate ways.

TEN MINUTES ON A SUNDAY MORNING IN JULY

A clear run of green lights all the way to the red one at
                                        Chiappini Street.
While I wait there I think again about the fact that A.A. Ball
are screw merchants painted on the corner wall.
Coming over the hill you can see foam dashing against
                                        Robben Island.
It looks like snow pouring out of the sea.
The water is a dark blue-green – a colour that may be
                                        called teal.

A cold-weather colour.

The woman walking towards the cars in the gutter
is the same one who's been living in alleys around here
for years: she looks as fit and graceless as ever,
better clothed than usual.

How could they have charged me only R3.30 for eight
                                        rolls and two cinnamon croissants?
He wanted to give me back my R4.00 as change, too.
We must both have been fast asleep.
Little girl, be grateful your mother has such long thin legs
in those black leggings. If I'd been able to inherit legs like that,
how my life would have changed.

There's another cold front rising up over the buildings
on the west side. Hope the rain comes this afternoon
so I can switch on the TV and forget
my unfinished conversation with you.
If you were home now I'd phone you but we never say those
                                        kinds of things
on the phone so there'd be no point.
I wonder if you heard me this morning.

You never were much good at physics

You never were much good at physics,
the non-metaphysical kind.

You wear me like a parachute
open wide, soft as silk,

no weight at all on your back
but there at the end of a forest of strings

holding you up while you steer yourself
and you're shooting holes in me

now, in your hunger for more of the sky
you're tearing my silk, you think all the holes

are good for us both, letting the sky in
to hold you up, tearing me open –
you think the sky is what holds you.

BREAKFAST

You've finished telling me what's going to happen to us.
You suggest we go for breakfast. The way you butter your roll
I can tell you're pleased with how the conversation went.

Across my eyes all possible words run.

My tongue numbs, my throat closes
while these words pour through my eyes,
desperate creatures running from a fire.

LOVE AND STORIES OF LOVE

Love is what stories of love leave out.

Love is always to one side, leaning against the wall
watching the love story act out completeness,
centrepiece of the party.

Love tends towards its story, asymptote with a twisted spine
drawn oppositely from its chosen axis.

Not a dog pining for you,
not a rope of pearls curled in your bag,
not a car willing to burn up carrying you through the desert.

A separate someone, closing its eyes near you,
your face like unplanned fingerprints all over its dreams.

IF HE'D BEEN CALLED JESSE

If he'd been called Jesse, or Jeremy,
we'd have understood him better,
the Jesus man from a world
where every tenth man was called Jesus.

Adonis, Romeo, Aphrodite,
how we've misspoken them all
in this English language that has no gods.
They were just guys and girls who shone a bit
more than their friends, but not so much more –
and so human, too, in their divine and gorgeous ways.

I've known two Cassandras,
both in the fashion business, one a good athlete as well.
How much more of the future did they see than I do,
and were they more powerless than me to change
                              any part of it?

Myths and religions in English
are always translated from somewhere else,
from worlds where they're old family tales
handed down, and everyone has a grandmother
who was once Delilah, an aunt with Medea's eyes.

LETTERS TO TOM

dear Tom
you sat in a Cape Town restaurant with me
and said
it's impossible to eat a sandwich with a knife and fork

therefore
this is for you

~

the truth is
we haven't a clue

well, not much of a clue

enough of a clue to get to the front door
but then what

~

through three winters
and three summers
and three autumns
and three springs
a torn black refuse bag
has hung from the plane tree's lowest branch
blowing itself to shreds
that stay stuck there

~

dear Tom
here we are again
tomorrow never comes
she'll be coming round the mountain
and I will always love you (no, not *you*)
dear Tom, in lower case luminosity

~

mistakes are made
of memories

head and heart
my tortoise and my hare
each under a lettuce leaf
praying for nightfall

~

tuning forks
refuse trucks
life on Mars
the flooded parking lot

~

too tired to rock and roll
too young to waltz
fast food will have to do

~

believe it or not
I know what I'm doing

~

dear Tom
I don't always know what you're on about
but thank you, this is oral poetry isn't it
I have to slow down and listen and imagine
a curved English accent
it frees me up I want to
play freecell now for a bit I think I have a cold coming
is it okay to do this? I think it is
reading you, the past seems boring my past
sentences I mean

on the page I'm in charge
I should have said
long ago
but I don't believe
even now it's true

twelve referees and a gatekeeper are lined up
along the margin
thumbing each line
      down
      down
      down
      up
gosh, really? thank you so much

     ~

I bet you'll have no idea what I'm on about
my voice isn't curved or English enough
or oral at all

come back sometime,
we'll make sandwiches

yours in a manner of speaking
as they say, Karen

REALLY, THERE'S NOTHING

Comets are massing on the borders of the sky
and there's nothing we can do to stop them.

This is the modern world,
the sky is blue, the coffee's brewing
and all day we can swim
and read the papers.

The comets are massing
without our assistance.

China has doubled its military budget,
Pakistan and Nigeria are discussing gunships.
America has them all covered, missile for missile.
South Africa sends planeloads of arms
on humanitarian missions to every continent.
Small non-aligned nuclear weapons wander the landscape
like innocent backpackers. Just looking.

In one small barn alone
ten million hens have died
without seeing the sun or stepping on soil.

In the shopping malls
weapons are sold
but may not be carried.

When they're ready the comets will burst
through the curtains
into your room.

No one will mind what you're wearing,
it's fine to sleep naked, spend the night smoking a joint,
watch the moon pass,
watch fireflies tease the rats.

Life is as beautiful as the glorious explosion
of a planet, the same sunset flare of colours,
the same tears of earth and water shrapnel
flying into the darkness, modern and ending.

A MAN WITH NO POWER

A man with no power can breed budgies,
build train sets that fill a dining room,
collect stamps
and take photographs.

He can read about cattle farming.
He can talk all night on a Citizen Band receiver,
and try to swop the Meccano set he bought his son
for a radio-controlled plane or boat or what-have-you.

A man with no power
will watch his children go out with their friends,
go to the beach, go to movies,
talk about countries they plan to hitchhike through
when they leave school.

He'll avoid his wife
who watches what he eats and what he wears.
He'll sit for hours in his car listening to the radio.

FAST ASLEEP

I'm lying in the sun reading poems about places full of
                                          dust and cars,
bushes and trains, birds and drunk rock 'n' roll fans,
lynxes and lonely poets.

Next to me you're fast asleep but your skin
knows where my arm is, you roll against it if I move
and your claws curl.

Later I look up, you've moved into the shade,
your eyes are almost closed, your long left paw
has stretched in my direction, waiting
for me to notice it.

Don't bother me, you say, turning your head to the side,
and when I pull my hand back you stretch your paw
                                          further towards me
and prod, and turn your head aside again
saying, don't bother me.

Odd calculus

Rewards
peculiarly valued.

A place in heaven.
A Mercedes Benz.

Is the difference that
heaven has place for everyone
but a Merc only seats five people?

Give a beggar R5 and you get into heaven.
But it costs R875 million in arms contracts to get a Mercedes

and even then they want to take it back from you.

ON FIRE

I was in the club, dancing, smoke drifting through my hair,
I was on fire, dancing, it was as dark as bass drums.
The boys have red razor wire eyes,
the girls flash their microwave lips.

It's so light, everyone shines in the darkness
bouncing and shouting, no one can hear,
the same words in the music, the same words
like hot steel flashing, like surgical knives,
everyone's dancing.

The boys have mud fingers, cracked raw,
the girls are sharpening their bones.
Outside the streets are dusty, old skin, torn hair.
In here there are no streets, everything shines,
in here it's melting with sex.

In the club I was dancing and freedom was growing fast
and still it continues to sharpen their bones
and they run through the city laughing,
their bright red laughter, their cavernous skin.

I want a drink, I don't care what's in it,
I want to dance. The room's dark,
I'm full of music, let's dance,
breathe on me.

Whipped cream

The Speaker is a meringue
with a spike through the middle.

The Deputy Speaker's a long chain of crystallised ginger
dipped in pepper and ground cloves.

The Chief Whip is a pair of pork pies
wrapped in laminated magazine pages.

And the MPs of the ruling coalition
clink clink clink clink
like chocolate coins in the President's pocket
ready to give to children at traffic lights.

Do you love yourself like this

Do you love yourself like this,
former warrior
bursting with luxury
in your narrow parliamentary seat?
Does your body enjoy being this big?

Did you imagine
it would turn out like this?
As you walk into court
between your lawyer and your wife
do you feel proud
of your arms-deal-payola 4x4?
Are you ready to die
to defend it
from being repossessed?

I hope so.
I hope this all has meaning for you,
this ugly life you've chosen
after so much struggle.

I want all people to be happy,
even you.
I hope you feel proud of yourself,
I do.
(Someone has to.)
You were so beautiful once.

~

You once had to try and survive
death by wet bag torture
and the knees of a man
in your kidneys, pressing harder, harder.

Does your car compensate for that?
Is that what makes you feel you deserve
the bespoke suit and shirt and tie
stretched tight around your swollen neck?

I worry that you'll think this question
snide or cynical. It isn't – I want to know
if that's the reasoning that works for your integrity.

Some people say
what you're doing now
simply confirms what your politics were
all along.

I'm not one of them –
I think, Stalinism and the sneering shadow flitting
                                    across your eyes
notwithstanding, that you had something to fight for,
something greater than clothes and a car,
more lithe, more radiant inside its own skin.
You were so beautiful then.

Hotel Rwanda, 1 January 2006

1

Men dancing in the streets with guns
and bright bandannas on their heads
and khaki shorts and cotton shirts
the colours of the summer fruits.

Men dancing in the streets with guns
and log-piled bodies on the verge
and long grass, summer's long grass starred
with red blood berries, whimpering breaths

hidden beneath the shady trees
like baby birds that tried to fly
but fell, fell to the soft wet soil,

whimpering breaths almost like names
or mewing kittens thrown away
by boys with pockets full of stones,

drowned in their laughter,
incinerated in the daylight's flickering red-rimmed eyes.

2

Why shouldn't the sins of the fathers be
visited upon their sons?

The fruits are,
the heroic myths are,
the promises are.

And all of these fell from a tree of sin
grown from the blood and muscle of others.

So let the sons have the skeletons in
                             their back yards,
let them find the ghosts in their passages,
let them hear the cries of the dead in
                             their sleep
and let these be indistinguishable
from the cries of their own children
who know what's coming for them
when history makes them men.

PRAISE POEM: I SAW YOU COMING TOWARDS ME

I saw you coming towards me
from far away.

From far away
I recognised you.

1   *I meditate on why your appearance is that of a good man*

Bear. No. Faithful St Bernard, gentle rescuer.
Are you coming to drag me to safety, to shelter me.

Your domed head, your shield of shoulders, arms –
symmetry of a father's boulder love.

Bare skull unafraid of the sky's temper.

They say you're a poor man, a man of the poor,
your hands have made your soul breathe.

St Bernard's steady gaze, stern with love.
No. Bear. Flint-eyed. Now I see
the grey glints there, they come from stone.
Dead stone splintering, flash of false fire.

2   *I meditate on what you have gathered to you and thrown aside in the course of your life*

Man walking towards me through valleys that throw
                              their shadows over you.
As you walk you grow bigger – are these your wives and
                    daughters spreading shadows around you.
Are these your lands and cattle, your brothers and sons.
Your eyes are the valley's wells, deepening as your smile spreads.

You are huge now you are a leader of people, your
                    shadow spreads wide like the rainclouds
we pray for that build and build until their grey swollen
                        thunder-laden hearts burst upon us
hail batters us water floods over us we lose our footing
                                    we must swim now
where the rain takes us our houses are broken planks
                            swimming behind us
and in the wet light of evening we see you have gone,
you have vanished into the place of secrets.

And you return, you return from that wilderness of
                            treachery and thorns
where you fought your war which now you bring back
                                to lay at our feet.
They say life was terrible there, they say you were the
                                one to fear,
commander of kindness and torment. Your body is
                hard like a drum beaten in victory.

Now you have found sunlight and a suited street to walk in,
where did you leave your valley promises.
Your body is rounded and full, did you eat them, did
                            you sell them.
Your dance is slow and deliberate, the street settles under it.

From your eyes I see that you own only this one suit
but you are glad of gifts, you wear them as if they were yours.

3   *I meditate on the beauty of distant danger*

Man of whirling scythes and knives,
feet in the soil, eyes caressing an army of young warriors

with whips and jungle pits
teaching them to turn their whimpering nightmares

into roars that can kill even the smallest creature,
make them cry in pain, show them

what it takes to break an enemy's spirit
and make him love you.

4   *I meditate on my own small imagination*

Kindness is all I can imagine, my weak arms know nothing
of the power I see rippling in you. I can't find my way
                                        through your heart,

doubts like a cloud of bees cover my face and I try to
                                        fold inward,
to become tasteless as stone, safe from my doubts and
                                            from you

coming too close, if your hand touches me
the pressure of your generous hand increases on me

– is this kindness? can I return your grasp?
I try to run into a cave of safety.

How beautiful your shadow is
spread across the mouth of my cave

still, still I want to see someone kind and strong
who will be on my side coming towards me

when you come looking for me
my cave shrinks, my dream of kindness
seems like embers of an old myth,
ash in my mouth.

5   *I meditate on tragic riddles*

A good man gets caught in a trap by evil forces that
                                        bring him down.
What's new?

Parsing the sentence:
how good?

was he caught or did he look for it?
was it a trap or a good idea?
how evil?
forces beyond one man's power to resist?
did the evil forces bring him down or was it something else –
                                        like good forces?
can a good man be brought down by good forces?
is he down or just floating between mountain peaks?

6   *I meditate on how you're just like all the others*

Versions of you

all collapse around that sentence:
He offered to massage her.

Every woman knows that moment
when honour throws off its cloak
and starts to take, take what it wants.

He offered to massage her.
He said: You must be cold, here let me –
He said: I just want to –
He said: You're so tense –
He said: Here baby –

Every woman knows that moment.

7   *I meditate on sand beneath the sea*

Where the tide has pulled back the sand is filthy
or so it seems, a grey-brown colour like polluted mud
streaked with crushed things that barely glint with
                                grains of mineral life.
Hours from now the water will return and what lies
                                there will sparkle
like a land of emeralds and pearls. It's only the
                                undrinkable water
that makes it shine like this, trickster sea, laughing at our thirst
with its delicious shimmer.

I'm just one of the dry shells under your feet,
so small you wouldn't notice me, maybe you'd grab at
                              me to pick your teeth
absently as you walk along, singing your ringtone song,
smiling at the boys who recognise you and call out your name.

I wish I were even smaller. I don't want to be seen,
                              touched, smiled upon
by you, coming towards me.

8   *I meditate on dreams come true*

He stands adored and steady
as a stone on a high mountain,
nothing holding him back from falling on us all.
Men cheer. Women cheer.

All the street lights bend their sodium crowns to greet you.
All the ragged boys acclaim your polished skin.

He is the son and father of their past,
he sings the songs they dreamed
would bring the stolen cattle home
and dances with the slow beat of a chief's heart

singing his way to the car with the tinted windows,
surrounded by warriors in black suits
and hidden eyes, spilling his song along the road
like cattle vanishing into the distant hills,
leaving oil streaks on the tar and a smell of burning tyres.

9   *I meditate on the power of art*

Make him a cloak of metaphors
stitched from the velvet napes of many cattle.
Praise him.
Create him anew.
Save him for history as he shrinks inside his suit.

Coda   Praise song for a man coming towards me

Once you came towards us bravely as rushing river water.
You flowed thunderously and sweetly towards us with
                                        your understanding.

Now you trickle through that same river bed
like the thinnest trail of spittle left by a sick man,
your roar clatters like pebbles thrown by boys into dry gutters.

Your breath sets fire to the frail crops.
Your feet stamp the floor of the house until it breaks open.

You whose blood is as dark as the blood of a lion
when it has been poisoned by honey from the hives of
                                        a nation,
eaten and spilled wide across the floors of so many houses –

on your way home you renounce the peacock's feathers,
                                        mocking them
and take for yourself the leopard's pelt as if it was your own.
See there where the peacock comes to meet you at your
                                        front door,
he will walk ahead of you to sing your coming,
you wear him alive and whole
and the leopard's corpse rots in the hearth, in your mother's
                                        hearth it rots.

Man who, when you come among us
makes our bodies seem to grow fat
and our clothes shine in your hot shadow,
but when you leave we see we are as thin as worn shafts
and our shirts have shrivelled to muddy rags.

Your legs had the strength of tree trunks when you
                                        strode towards us
but now they are shrivelled, you are a man walking on old
                                        canes chewed by rats.

Man of three legs standing astride our land like the feast pot
you make us believe we can kill hunger while you rise over us
but you eat your food yourself, your shadow fattens
while we watch with wide mouths.

You landlord of the dreams of people,
hunter of our hopes who captures them
like an old bear that can no longer eat,
eagle with the ragged beak of a vulture –
beware the winter hour when your wings fail you,
beware the hungry boys with stones waiting
in the street where you will land, where you will wander
                                              whimpering
among the piles of refuse left by your armies.

I saw you coming towards me
from far away.

From far away
I recognised you.

Mnemonics

1

Cool and shadowy, the corridor between the beach huts
where the sand is always damp —

such a sweet place for six-year-old feet
safe from the white-hot sand
on the wide beach where the aunts sit
spreading their pink lipstick and diamonds

and the glutinous seabed naked at low tide,
dimpled with bluebottles wetly wriggling
around a little girl, her long wail
as a stranger dabs vinegar on her ankle.

2

The wet scent of oleander leaves
under the hosepipe's spray

while I play beach bats on the garden path
with my teenage cousin, scraping the plastic bat
against the stones, beating him,

noticing as I lunge for the ball
that I'm laughing, knowing I'll remember

that I was being a happy child.

3

Mince that was fine-grained and spicy, pillowed
inside fluttering pastry, its translucent underbelly

hot, soft in our fingers.
Only my brother and I remember

those pies from the Danish Kitchenette
and the quiet woman who made them,

serving two shy children gently
as if they were her only customers.

4

A dog's frantic claws scrabbling on a steel table,
like my dog's claws,

her head twisted towards me
as I left the surgery.

And at home the way they all turned away
because I'd done what they told me to

and come back alone. Now, even now, my hand clenched,
that should have kept stroking her.

A CHILD CAN'T BE BORN

A child can't be born
knowing who suffered for his birth

and how old must he be
before he can utter his first

no to the safety stolen
from others for him?

His mind is panes of glass stained
all the colours of his days and nights –

where does he find that one colour
he has never seen,

the one whose name is
no, not this?

In Cameroon, August 2005

approaching a stranger
approaching a strange place

this is like
this isn't like

the ordinary things people do there,
the Sunday things, the Monday things

I marry my strangeness to yours,
foreigner in a foreign country

we're different in the same measure
that we're the same, what marks us

are the things that place you on a soft path between palm trees
carrying a child on your back

and me on a terrace overlooking an ocean,
filtering words through wet light

your other child was walking with an armful of
                                        sandwich loaves
like the ones I ate when I came home from school

does he like peanut butter?
do you wish he'd eat yams instead?

I want them to cook plantain for me here
and they ply me with omelettes and pasta

the man who followed you up the hill
is following me back down

and each of us steps into a room
as the wind rises and the phone rings

to bring news of a person who's dying where I come from
like the old man I see through a window in your house,
                              weeping from milky eyes

later I see you staring at the grey light that is both sea and rain
where the equator hovers, it's right here, close enough to touch

THE POOL ATTENDANT AT THE FIRST INTERNATIONAL INN IN LIMBÉ

The pool attendant
at the First International Inn in Limbé
is called Eugene Douné.
He introduces himself on my third morning there
and asks for some paper to write down his name
and telephone number (00237 2217435).

He tells me how often he cleans the pool and the patio around it.
We sit together for a while without speaking,
watching the grey Atlantic Ocean and the surly tankers coming in
from France and America to load oil at the refinery
on the spit of land just beyond the beach.
The warm rain falls without a break
onto his swimming pool.

Between us it is understood
that he dreams of coming to my country
and that I'll carry his phone number back there,
and if ever I see a way to bring him to South Africa
to find work like his excellent pool-cleaning work here,
or something else he can try,

I'll telephone him at once.

THE QUALITY OF POSTCARDS

The quality of postcards in poor countries is different.
They always seem much handled, like old photographs
taken by someone who knew and loved this lake,
this volcano, this man on a bicycle,

scruffy at the edges, the colours faded,
slightly softened by damp,
as if they've been carried around in someone's pocket
for many years and taken out often to look at

but must now be sold to tourists
who won't stay long enough to make their own
postcards of the landscape around them,
step by step along the road of living here.

Is someone mourning for these cards,
sold to pay for something more needed?
Are they all that's left of a vanished person's life,
abandoned on a dusty floor in an old hut?

In rich countries the postcards are better than the real scenes,
glossier, less windy, brilliantly coloured
as if no one ever scuffed up the soil with her footsteps

or smudged the sky with a finger sticky with berry juice
while making these private notes,
reminders of the world still here
that no camera could colour correctly.

ELAINE'S GARDEN

1

You lived in a dry place and watered it carefully.

I always brought flowers
to thank you,
to wish you happiness.

Nothing else seemed light enough.
Flowers expect to be thrown away,
no sin, no shame.

To know another person is not mysterious.
But to touch her is forbidden.

2

I look up now and then and

there you are,
half-turned from the kitchen towards the lounge,
mug of tea in your hand.

there you are,
walking in your slow way between the girls' room and yours,
something on your mind that you won't utter.

there you are,
in the yard, moving between the washing lines
                              and the back fence,
checking on something, fetching in the dry sheets.

That's all you do
and you keep doing it,
I'm keeping you there.

3

What to do when a person dies
who never told you her secrets:
paint her as she walked towards you,
smiling as she wanted you to see her smile.

4

Scattered around the city
your daughters and their daughters cry for you,
remembering that you said you were tired,
tired of it all, the girls with their babies,
the clothing accounts, the stray boys at the fence,
your body, demanding a kind of care
you didn't have to give.

You knew it would just go on.
They watched you turning away,
moving more slowly,
couch to sun porch,
porch to corner chair,
chair to bedroom
to lie down
just for a while.

5

In every house
there's a woman like you,
standing the way you do, at an angle to the room,
keeping it steady without seeming to,
pillar, brace, stay,
wearing old cotton, vigilant,
walking slowly from room to room
resting only the way the walls of a house rest.

Around you young women and small boys dart and flutter
or come to cling to your shadow for a moment.

You say no, and the fluttering young women run off
shouting yes, but come back bruised and crying.
The young boys fall asleep in your lap.

Winter by winter a blanket of permanence spreads from your eyes
through the house, the rooms fold themselves around
                                        each Sunday lunch.

Your summers are warm doorways where you sit,
                              smoking a cigarette,
watching the street beckon your children.

6

You've chosen a quiet vanishing,
letting first speech, then sight, then touch
leave the room,
letting the soft conversations of neighbours and friends
wash your cold skin.

By the time I come you're spending the heartbeats
of your last slow day of breath.
I stand in your doorway, then leave.

This time I've brought armloads of jasmine and buddleia from
                                        my spring garden,
knowing their scent is too heavy for your daughters
crowded together making sandwiches for a vigil,
letting the flowers scatter and drown in their buckets of water,

letting me pass through, as you always did,
turning gently away.

7

The young ones have no language for what's happening
and hold their own breath,
saving it for the wild howl they need
when you leave at last,
leave your own bed, deathbed, warm bed
of your dead body close to everyone –

these lost girls in their black sandals,
finding their faces suddenly grave and stiff,
walking in a prayer-spattered circle
around the open coffin full of you,
walking in a wobbling line out into the icy sunshine

and you not there to call them
back across the street, back home.

8

The house stands trembling
like a dream emptied of its voice.

When will the roof fall,
how long can it hold its breath?

Your girls dance around inside like butterflies,
hovering against the windows
they used to dream of breaking,

the open windows they won't fly out of,
beating themselves instead against the glass
where your fingerprints still touch them.

Here is a basket of ironing,
here is a baby boy,
here is a group of young women
turning magazine pages.

9

People whose daily presence never changes
are the hardest ones to lose,

as if the earth has tilted
and you keep falling away from it.

10

I say, I want to plant something outside the front door
that spreads and flowers, in memory of you.
Your brother says, no one will take care of it,
they're not interested.

He's probably right.
But I want that garden for you
that you would have refused,
I want you to come out here
and stand next to me and smile at what grows here,
its perfumed colours spilling over you.

11

Dear Elaine
this is all (I can say),
this is all.

THREE MEDITATIONS ON IMMORTALITY
OR
ARE WE NEARLY THERE YET?

The soul must be the bones,
since they're what lasts
forever and ever, stark and serene.
Where else would a soul want to live?

It must have happened
at least once in all the aeons
that a clutch of turtle bones tumbling
in the deep currents formed themselves
into a perfect model of the Parthenon.

~

What happiness, to be folded in the soil's arms
through rain and drought,
to wear a cloak of laced roots and beetle husks,
to sleep so safely, undisturbed
and always with earth's tiny rivers of air
whispering downward over you and through you,
as if you were their best route to the sea.

~

After the careful flatness of the years
of skin walls holding you in
now the action starts:

wild body bursting forth with all its chemistry ablaze –
newborn star, climactic circus act,
whole tribe of tigers leaping out of the forest, roaring.

Three meditations on Why is there war, Mummy?
or
Against the hyper-legibility of the violent act

Maybe
if I was very hungry
or bored,
   bored, bored, bored
   itchy, acid edge on my skin,
maybe
I'd rip the legs off a country
one day, because there it was,
and I could.

~

Shoot.
A complete action.

Cock.
Pull.
Flash.
Bang.
Corpse.

Smoke halo
slowly dispersing.
(Inside me.)
The flat horizon, endless.

Have a smoke, a drink.
Sleep now, it's done.

~

What next?
Still so much of the day
to get through.
Start by sticking a knife in here, perhaps.
See what trickles out.

THE LAST THRESHOLD

The last threshold lies
in the eyes of the little boy
who watches his father come at him
with a belt.

THE PASSIVITY OF THE SPECTATOR MUST BE COUNTERED AT ALL COSTS

No better than tins of middle-cut tuna
opened on the theatre seats, smelling worse
as the heat of the performance flows over them,
say the theorists of participatory practice.
Solid chunks floating in salt water, long dead.

Not the cherry tomatoes they feel like,
these spectators bursting with their own flavour,
their tight skins glowing in the light
that reaches them from the stage,

dreaming their realest selves to life
in the spectacle laid out for them –
in good faith, they thought,
they thought they'd come to inhabit it –

but apparently they're not really alive here,
not really listening and watching,
not really wondering how it will all turn out.

Get them up.
Make them walk around, bump into each other.
Make them behave like real people in a real street
walking around, bumping into each other.

THIS IS THE BIT WHERE YOU LIVE

This is the bit where you live.
Dog sorrow, cat sorrow, rain on a closed window
and a whimpering hunger that climbs into you
and won't go away.

This is the bit where your heart aches
like a normal person, you find out
how the world turns grey when you're cast out into it,
how every day you have to attend your own funeral again.

Now and again this must be done,
this needing, this pleading for something
and hearing the word 'no'.

Now and again you must walk out into a freezing night,
pour out sounds without any rhythm
and lie down in them, like a real person
without any shelter.

LITERARY BIOGRAPHY OF THE NOBEL PRIZE-WINNING POET

He wept privately for years after his mother died, then
                                his father, then his brother.
Numerous servants and neighbours confirmed this.

He and his longstanding partner slept in separate beds
                                after the first few years.
Eventually they married. They squabbled over small things.

He often gave money to friends in difficulty,
or helped them when their cars were stuck.

Attending an exhibition opening of a close friend in 1963
he wore a brown corduroy jacket and pants with turn-ups.

OUT ON THE OCEAN

In the end it's enough
just to talk to a few other poets,
the ones you don't meet, who don't want to know
what you think of their poems.

The divorce of Tom Cruise and Nicole Kidman
is the kind of resource people need
to anchor their emotions and their imaginations.

Sitting alone in the middle of the ocean
repairing our nets, we're no use
and no loss to anyone.

Thank you, Ryuichi Tamura.
I've spent this hour among your lines
testing the pull of the spaces between them,
feeling the shapes of the white stones and the dark stones
you've collected. Separate and far away from everyone,
connected to everything human
this way.

Out on the ocean your stones skim past me,
touching three times before they disappear.

CLOSER THAN THIS

Extracts from a source book for urban planners

And on the eighth day

Someone said –
we'll have a city here
(town, township, settlement, whatever)
pointing at a blank spot in his eye,
his finger dripping decrees onto
whatever lay beneath it,

and you were standing
just to one side of where the decrees fell,
maybe you were reading a novel or counting birds,
or thinking of how to fit utopia through the eye of a storm,
but the decrees ran towards you following the incline of the land,
they pooled at your feet, your face was reflected in them –

what did you do?

Connected

In my room I hear the boy upstairs whose mother died
lifting weights and dropping them onto the floor above my head,
the mongrel puppy snuffling at the skirting board next door,
back and forth, back and forth, hungry for them to come home,
the white-eyes strung along the plane tree branches
chattering to the pearl-pink sky.

~

No closer than this.

~

Your shoulder falls against me in the taxi
and I can't think of it as innocent
but in your eyes I see that this is all you have to offer
though your hands are hardened like a farmer's shoes.

Poor man, I think, poor man.
What would you do with a small animal if it nudged your calf?
What would you do if I leaned against you
and said, tell me a story?

~

No closer than this.

~

The little girls know not to touch anyone.
Their mothers fold their arms as I walk past, turning away.

Young men shove their hands through the taxi window
to offer me keyrings and sunglasses.

'For home for away' they call, laughing,
they shout at me as we drive on.

~

No closer than this.

The things that survive
are the things that survive

Put a frame around it and it stops jiggling,
takes on proportions and resonances.

Take the frame away and it weathers into dirt.

The frame is just a rectangle of wood or metal,
mass-produced.

The jiggling was going to stop anyway, for a while.

When it starts up again it's heavier-footed
until the air gets hold of it, then it's grave dirt

dug up and drying out, the portion displaced
by the beloved body

with nowhere to settle
roaming in the air, surviving
or not.

The city turns the land
from an animal into a machine.

Statistics South Africa says

Statistics South Africa says there are 10,771 disabled people
in Khayelitsha.
Were. In 2001, or possibly 1996.

Of which a quarter can't see well,
a quarter can't move well,
three hundredths can't hear well,
a tenth can't think well,
thirteen hundredths can't feel well,
one twentieth can't speak well,
and nearly one tenth struggle with many of the things
humans are supposed to be able to do.

And according to Statistics South Africa there are,
were, 328,997 people living in Khayelitsha.
More or less.

Which would mean that for every disabled person
there are:
30.54 people to take care of them
7.98 households in which they might live
9.03 children who might look at them with wide eyes
0.68 pensioners who might spend time talking to them.

Wait a minute: 7,371 pensioners
in the whole of Khayelitsha?
I don't think so.

Anyway.
Here on a folding chair in the sun outside a house
looking onto the street a woman sits who may be one
of the quarter, the thirteen hundredths, the twentieth,
the nearly one tenth, or the 30.54 who watch over
someone not fully able to live
on the busy streets of a town no one can count properly.
She leans her head back against the wall so that the brick heat
can massage her crown and smiles.
For what it's worth she lives here, you can count her in.

A child walking past looks up from her cell phone,
her bright eyes register that the woman is not her mother or aunt,
her dark eyes busy far behind the bright eyes register
                                        without speaking
that she will be this woman one day,
they programme in the folding chair
in the sun against the wall overlooking the street.
What to expect, what to save up for.

No point counting.
The sums perpetuate themselves hand-to-hand.
The one who can't move now has her 30.54 people
remembering her hour after hour as they step around her,
                                over her, walk the other way,
drop blankets at the door.
The one who can't speak has 9.03 children's laughter
                                to scar him with sound.
The troubled thoughts of the one for whom
7.98 households stand ready will flow like a river through them,
and all their troubled thoughts will flow with him out
                                        into the streets
where children on their cell phones avoid the eyes of the pigeons,
kicking them with their little feet,
storing up data for long-term recall.

Unplace

What to do with four million people wandering around
all day with nothing to do?
This is not a statistic it's a mass of plankton with no
algae to eat,
a herd of lion cubs growing bigger by the hour,
a sea of hunger and boredom washing up against the
walls of every building.

City of aimless adults
pacing the same grooves into the same pavements hour
after hour.
Would a free museum on every corner help?
A library, a cinema, a sports café?
A gym with swimming pool?
A hobby centre with free tools and materials?

City of girls and boys full of bounding energy and curiosity
pacing up and down the sandy roads where no one
invites them in to play.
Would a military training programme help?
A 24-hour dance venue on every block?
Free sandwiches and apples for anyone willing to stay
off drugs?

It seems the city is not designed for people to just be
present in, Zen-like, still.
A useless location for foraging, for exercising the body,
for meditating on nature and god. No bible came from a city,
no moral teachings.
Send them back into the deserts and forests, the ones
with no jobs,
let them start their own cities, there's always room for a
new civilisation to start up
against a bare mountain, bare-handed and free of refuse
collectors, traffic police, housing authorities.

City streets

A woman drives with a faint smile on her face
just in case, just in case.

A man drives with a scowl on his
to show that he could, if you pushed him.

To love it

To love it you must be left alone there,
stand in its doorways, feel its despair touch your ankles
                                        and pass on,
find the warm room where strangers seem happy
to let you be, the room where music you've heard before
shows you where to sit, where to settle
for the duration.

To love it you must have time there
without words, without indoor escapes from its noise and dirt,
time with your own reflection in shop windows,
your thighs balanced between leather bags and ancient
                                        chess sets,
your face squeezed between piles of small batteries
and children's pencil cases and a chain of bird cages
                        knocking against your temples,
time learning how fast the cars turn the corner
and where the smell of urine settles.

To love it it's enough to find a pair of streets
that are awake when you are,
and one old man who sits in a shop
reading his newspaper as you pass by,
and two young women leaning against a wall, smoking.

Then you can come back,
when the time is right you can come back
to pick up where you left off,
the way people do who were always friends,
perhaps once lovers, too.

Typology

City 1 won't let you sit down.
City 2 says wear heavy shoes.
City 3 sends you across your own direction.
City 4 says whatever, just hurry up.
City 5 stands you against a wall.
City 6 follows your lead.
City 7 says never mind, have an orange.
City 8 asks you for a ticket.
City 9 touches you too quickly.
City 10 sits on the pavement watching you.
City 11 is ready for action.
City 12 wants you, but doesn't know how to ask.

The urban planner ruminates

After the first whisky

All the arguments have already been used up.
Everyone knows why it won't work
to give everyone a small kind house
or to ban shopping centres
or to let the roads be marked out by children playing
                                        adventure games.

It's naïve and also boring to ban cars and swimming pools
from cities and their suburbs, to ban suburbs,
to insist that everyone has to plant ten trees per year as
                                        a tax payment,
to encourage dogs to settle where once were tanning parlours.

Sometimes just
any place that shuts
any room, dry enough
walking distance from food and water.

Sometimes just
any place where you don't have to bargain, vote, explain,
make friends in order to stop moving on,
greet ten people in order to sit looking at a bush.

(No one celebrates bushes in memories of a place, isn't it odd,
always a tree or a hill or some climbing twisting thing, never a
simple bush sitting steadily on its own feet not even flowering
for attention.)

If everyone got a room and a good bathroom
no questions asked,
would that take the pressure off the capitalist system
to trade in homes?

If every square metre came with fibre optic connections
and a good bathroom, would we all just sit quietly for a bit
thinking, chattering in that wonderfully silent electronic language
that makes us invisible to the neighbours?

And then outside, cobbles for sentimental reasons, flowerbeds,
paths leading to little shops, children hopscotching to
                    keep the psychologists happy,
cats sunning themselves and dogs padding along being alert,
men sitting at tables in the sun, women learning to do the same,
would that satisfy the urban theorists?

Same old same old.

Everyone wants to live in pretty Minerve
the way it was before the market went global,
before all that blood flowed that makes the summer
                         geraniums glow
so firmly on their blond steps up to the little doors,
the good old thick doors with their cast iron hinges and
                         the lintels worn by hands,
real human hands now long dead, little children and
                         women and sturdy men
who ran through the streets screaming and then bled
                         into the earth,
bright Minerve with its vineyards and chateaux
is a place that shows how a place should be, a public private place,
a human place between hills and a gorge good for
                    defence, though too little in the end
to last when people came, real people on horseback
                    with vats of oil and swords
made in another town somewhere along the same road
with its church at a slightly different angle to its market square.

After the third whisky

What came first, the 'trinkets and baubles'
or the appetite for them?

If no one wanted them there'd be no shopping
and therefore no capitalism.

Cats like trinkets and baubles
at least for thirty seconds,

so do elephants, probably,
and moths, who like them big and blazing hot.

Must be an evolutionary thing,
trinket as food source perhaps or
bauble as shelter from the storm
or sweets for my honey,
sugar for my gene pool's mum –

not a sign of anthropo-spiritual genius but a DNA moment
prodding the creature into action –
maybe that's what all the junk DNA is for,
to spur the hunt for junk –

if stomachs get hungry, so do brains and fingertips
yearning for shiny fluffy silky glittering doses of sensory input.

Even Mr and Mrs Feudal Serf in their mud-spattered
                              clogs and coarse hessian coats
must have lifted their heads in longing when a crown rode by
(else why was it worn, the headache-inducing
                              spine-crushing crown
with its load of trinkets and baubles?).

Capitalism wouldn't have got started if the first peasant
                              had walked past
the first silver buckle displayed in the first shop window thinking,
what would anyone want with a thing like that?

And here we are, building gherkins and sailing ships
                              out of stone and glass
to amuse ourselves because there's nothing to watch
                              on television,
the wonderful city is too easy to explain,
its CAD-infused skin has no perfume,
what can we do next with our hands and eyes
to keep us out of trouble?

Uses of useful plants

One of the uses of useful plants
is to take less water than useless plants
so that the useless plants can survive.
Jacaranda. Lilies. Wisteria.

The one who dies

When the one who dies
was always a disappointment,

so many decades of hope
you have to set aside,

when you lift up each bright silk hour she offered you
and remember the shadow that made you step away

thinking better not this,
smile, leave now –

when the one who never was what the story promises
walks out of it finally, your grief flails like an unmoored sail

in strange crosswinds, and you find you have kept moving
                              beyond her harbour,
surrounded by flickering lights you wish were memories.

TANGO FOR PERSON AND CITY

Abrazo

If this is a tango
it is slow and warm
for an afternoon, pushing the windows open
onto familiar weeping pepper trees and traffic streams
then cold, spinning from one corner to another
of the wind.

Salida

The air falls in drifts
around us like clear snow:
this is the freeze and glide tango of winter.

And there are nut-brown rats
scampering around the crumbling *grands maisons,*

no fear, no harm, they vanish
fleet-footed among the crusts of old stucco –

fleeting, a word for you, this first encounter –
where are you?

What brushes against my hand
is only my own jacket, half-open.

Amagues

The man in his black wool coat and brown cigar
leaning against his black car
in the tiny street outside a brass-edged door
that could lead to a private bank,
a primary school,
a police intelligence bureau,
a perfect brothel,

the tired apartment of his dying mother,
turns his face away as I pass.

Volcadas

Hibiscus pink and pretty is the Casa Rosada,
and cornice-laden in the style of buildings
where the corridors are darkest.

Today the only mothers on the Plaza de Mayo
are foreign, shepherding their scrappy children
across the grass between statues, plaques
and stone-faced pigeons.

An army of radio masts observes them
from surrounding rooftops.

The friendliest things are
the poles at traffic lights and bus shelters
you can lean against, trying to refold
your map in the wind.

Baldoso

These were once the municipal food halls.
Today linen shirts and silver dinner bells
spill across the market tables,
basted by trays of monogrammed cutlery
and pop art sunglasses, and a giant Duracell bunny.

Hacienda curtains float like harlot ghosts in the draughty aisles
between beef aprons and meadows of clay buttons.

For me silk panels
fall from a rail,
crocus petals of a swirling skirt,
scarlet, tangerine, lavender veils.

Children running on rude feet
carve trails of rattling cups and saucers
along the weary floors.

Caricias

Little leftwing spinach pies
laced with nutmeg cheese
are so fragrant on paper plates

and a cloud of questions floats
over the cups of maté –
are you Zulu?
do South African workers have unions?

The kindness of foreign comrades
is a sweetness all of its own.

Caminando

The last men of the day
manoeuvre the last deliveries
through lukewarm doors.

At the corners black bags pile and settle
spilling food only half-soiled,
shredded paper, metal bones,
thin rivulets of liquid that shine
blond, then red
in the late light.

Two bodies lay themselves down in an entrance way
and cover each other with newspapers,
becoming this night's warm replicas of the heroes
standing in grey alcoves nearby –
they are my landmark on endless Independencia,
the sign that this is the place to turn
for the street where my bed is tonight,
Las Piedras, Street of Stones.

Golpecitos

Above the counter the menu speaks
International McDonald's
modestly, not pointing out
that this is the inner core of the global nuclear reaction
we know as forest-stripping-climate-change-inducing-
dollar-parity-setting-McDonald's-burger-
beef-production, Argentina.

At eye level there are trays
of fresh breakfast pastries
with tastes and shapes unnameable
north of the Amazon basin.

I don't speak Spanish,
the waitron doesn't speak English.
I'm trying to buy a second cup of coffee.
She's trying to tell me I get a free refill.
Words and smiles fluttering helplessly
over the empty mug.

I give up and return to my table.
Her colleague appears at my elbow
with a full pot, freshly made.
All is clear, all is kind.

Two bag ladies with separate mouthfuls of muttering
leave holding paper cup refills,
the rumpled pacing man in half a uniform
gets a fresh pastry
and returns to his up and downing the narrow aisle,
frowning and chewing.
Safe here on this Sunday-lonely morning
we all are.

Cadencias

And there's your tango, in the tourist street,
man with a life-size cloth doll lady
that makes no effort to look real,
staring the laughing tourists down
with a tango designed to show them
something unkind about life,
about streets full of dancing couples.

Molinete

But your true home, the Café Tortoni,
is beautiful still in its *beaux arts* glow
and the gentle waiter in his professional soul
laughs at our mistrust, remembers everything we ask for,
smiles at the guest who wants
artichoke salad and hot chocolate,
makes the room seem as though it belongs to him, to us,
to any vagrant guests who have lived elsewhere
as he lives here.

Cruzada

When the bosses ran north carrying
all the dollars in the bank,
the Chilavert print shop workers took ownership
of the plant and its elegant books and nervous clients
not without struggle, but in the end
here they are at midnight performing their triumph
among the sleeping machines, it's freezing,
the factory floor erupts in song and
turns silent as the play introduces a virgin bride
in a white gown, like a ghost her tears grow flames
as she becomes pure rage, the walls glimmer
with holograms of all the gods and elders
who enchain her, they transmute by unknown power
into dancing prisoners and labourers
and will it work? will it work?

The audience applauds, throws coins and notes
into the basket passing down the rows, hugs all the actors
and heads for the empty street to hunt for taxis,
it's really cold out here.

Hours later, huddled under a borrowed blanket,
so glad to have reached this bed at last,
to be indoors, even wide awake
and shivering from a cold water bath,
I offer thanks to the resident cat
padding delicately across my suitcase.

Resolución

I can't say you held me close,
it was the first time.

One afternoon you put your arm around me,
the next day it was the narrow street again,
buses brushing my shoulders aside.

There was no promise
to meet again.

DEER ON THE FREEWAY

Driving on the freeway near midnight
I saw a young deer stand suddenly on the verge
and step forward into my lane,
as if this was Norway, as if I was walking
in a winter story in the nineteenth century.

At 80 km/h you must keep going if you can,
swerve only slightly,
hold your lights steady.
The deer was still, alert, not yet alarmed.

Others saw it.
For a moment a spirit of carefulness spread among us,
four cars with four drivers moving separately towards the city,
each slowing like someone entering a forest of sleeping children,
awake in a new way, fearful of doing harm,
grateful for the care that others took.

Everyone knows what it means,
a young deer appearing in a city
unafraid, quietly standing on the road
as cars speed towards it.

Riffs for the caring girl

who's small and thin-limbed inside her whatever body
unvarnished, freckled with old skin and dust

so young, so young no matter what
whose dreams are poor, whose weariness

turns to daydreams when the sun shines, who feels
exactly what each suffering person feels

who knows what happiness would look like
because she saw it dancing past one day

who wants to be kind and every hour
anger drowns her kindness in its brine

who can't help anyone to stay alive
although she tries and tries

who cries because she feels love when a dog nuzzles her –
riffs for the caring girl

who's still at sixty holding up her raving daughter
and consoling her mother for a life without radiance,

who looks at magazine stories of happiness found at last
by women so much younger than herself

and wonders how it's possible to have said yes to everything
and still missed the door out of her body into the room

where a man waits for her with his arms open, surely
she tried to find him, surely she did?

~

the caring girl is little like a fan in someone's hand
washing and washing the hot skin where fever grows
wilder and more determined with each split and bloom of cells

her back is straight
her stories hold the daylight still

until the sick man shudders
at their too much brightness

so she blows her voice out,
lets the silence vanish her

now she's only air, cooling air

~

everything depends on how many routes you open up
                                        at the beginning,
how many roads out how many taste sensations how
                              many adventurous starts
with no idea what happens next

and if like the caring girl the number is none at all
because no one gets hurt or asks questions if you're
                                        sitting there
quite visible, head in a book
and no one will cry from loneliness or curse you
because you weren't there when needed

then afterwards that's what's possible

~

and what is the thing the caring girl longs for?
surely there must be such a thing

and there is —
a strong man, a gentle man,
what some would call a Hollywood fantasy,

or if they were kind a father-figure,
a man to love her, hold her
and tell her three precise things:

you're the most beautiful person I've ever met
I love you, only you
I'll look after you forever

these three small wishes
sit on the caring girl's lips
and she knows (how does she know?)
they're wrong,
that no one gets this,
that strong young men die
in a pool of their own faeces,
or become rabid predators with guns
to shoot those who care most for them,
or just vanish, just vanish

so behind these three wishes
is a fourth wish,
a wish that knows it is a curse
but stoically chooses itself to be the real wish:

to not want anything from any man or woman,
to be at peace with the dry ground and the cold water of solitude
and die like the small winds that leave before anyone
                                    feels them and looks up

            ~

take some risks
the words fly from some radio talk show
straight towards her

the only risk she can imagine
is to keep on walking
away from home,
along a road that goes on forever
as far as she knows

in a similar landscape

no surprises there

still – she went further than she would normally
past her Monday, past her washing line

and was she
raped and murdered walking across a field/
spotted by a modelling agent from his car/
shot by a stray bullet/
picked up by a couple who collect rural women to sell
                                    as maids in town/
chased by a dog off a farm/
fed by a Christian tourist/
left alone/

a pile of grey-skinned sorrow at the side of the road
a sunbird pecking at a hotel tree

let's hear it for the caring girl
wherever she may be

              ~

let's hear it for the caring girl,
mother of all social workers and white weddings
possessed of a heart that contracts in pain
at the sight of any child or adult crying
evolved for this purpose
miracle of anthropic necessity
sine qua non of civilisation

GREAT AND TRUE

Everyone agreed
there should be a novel
of the third kingdom,
preferably in the form
of a film,
or a song,
though no one was
sure what it should be about
or when,
when the third kingdom
would have come
or when it would
go, and leave them
with a novel,
the novel,
the one that was
great and true, preferably
in the form of
a familiar truth
or at least
a nice one.

Phendukani Silwani

His name is Phendukani Silwani.

He was made of carbon and light
and has vanished forever.

~

Phendukani's voice, flying home from school
ahead of him one kilometre after another,
crossing the river, finding stone after stone in the cold water,
fetching his friend, his other friend, his dog
in from the hills to walk with him
through the bushes, one kilometre after another,

little boy on your way home —
'Where are you? I'm here. Where are you?'

~

His vanishing was efficient,
it barely scratched the air of the country.

His life endures forever
only here, where his footprints
sparkle in the river's memory.

~

Phendukani can write the alphabet and numbers.
He can tell a story on the classroom magic carpet,
he can kick a ball hard enough to hurt his foot but not the wall.
He hasn't grown into his knees yet.
In the ground they'll lie like scaffolding for an unbuilt tower.

In the magic carpet there's a hole
each child falls through, remembering Phendukani,
falling into the mists of *Come unto me,*

following his voice with theirs
to weave a nest of hymns his spirit can fly home to.

~

Phendukani on a horse
panting through the beautiful valleys
to find a nurse, a doctor, a car,
turned back at the boundary
between the land and the highway.

Small saddlebag of life
slumped across the horse's patient back
nowhere to go but home
to the house that freedom has not blessed

hunched against his father's chest
holding his pain steady, borrowing the horse's breath
and his father's heartbeat to reach the last day of his life.

~

In the shadow of the broken house
those who love him stand together
to bury his burst body, shrouded
in death's cold exhausted air.

On the horizon the Ministers pause to wish them well.

~

When a child dies, who is responsible?
It's a complicated diagnosis.

When his liver turns against him,
who can say what story it has to tell,
what its tumours remember?

~

Let Phendukani Silwani stand for all Departments of Health,
all out-patient queues and closed wards and unbought
                              drugs and spent doctors.

Let Phendukani Silwani stand for all Departments of Education,
all unbuilt schools and untrained teachers and stolen food
                              and books bearing false witness.

Let Phendukani Silwani stand for all Departments of Housing,
all cracked walls and broken pipes and poisoned streets
                              and lost gardens.

~

Phendukani is playing with an old tin and some wire.
And then he is not.

Phendukani is brushing his teeth.
And then he is not.

Phendukani is calling goodbye as he turns the corner.
And then he is not.

~

Let Phendukani Silwani stand for all parents
with emptied arms and bent heads
whose tears hang like silver nooses in the air.

Let him stand for all children,
all parcels of carbon and light
who come only once, and vanish forever.

~

Let Phendukani Silwani stand for himself only,
only he existed in his small body,
only he was there, looking out at us,
at the tall grass that hid him,
at the unreachable blue sky.

~

Thank you for the Paracetamol.
Thank you for the social grant.

POEM FOR WHICH THERE WAS NO TITLE

Yes,
I've said yes
to you,
to going
as far as I must
with you.

~

When I first saw you,
fabled visitor to our fabled land,
you were as real as a table or a chair
and it made perfect sense
that you were sitting there
with my name in your hands.

Over tea and *petits fours*
in the olive plush chairs
in front of the Pompeii mural

we had an entire conversation without a sound
while your minders mapped and folded
your coming days and nights.

By the time you left
we'd laid that journey to rest
and embarked on our own one
to be continued

(dangerously –
this that we'd started
a dare thrown down
between our discreet shoes:
never show,
never tell,
never say
it wasn't real
enough).

By the time I left there
on my own I realised
I'd fallen down a rabbit hole
and you were the one come to catch me
and keep falling with me.

~

Old enough to know
this is worth risking everything for.
Old enough to know
what's done is done

and this is new,
this is the next spring
that comes and I could hope
it will be the last, the longest one.

~

When you fetch me
remember to do it silently
so that no one will know

and when you bring me back
remember to do it without a word
so that I won't find out until long after.

~

Your hands, your stranger's hands –
watching them move
my wrists move,
my ribs open,

and then your eyes – they know
everything I know,
and what will come of it –

unsmilingly
you dare me to go further,
you promise nothing,

looking directly at me
you see the thing
I almost have a name for

flickering inside, catching, burning.

~

A thousand people have a claim on you
but you have a claim on me.

A hundred thousand queue outside your sleep
but you knock gently at my door
and yes, yes
I permit you to enter.

~

Everything was
preparation
for this.

All the tears and fevers,
all the cold cement survivals
are over.

Don't wait,
don't wait any longer.

~

Don't worry,
I've covered your tracks
though not my own.

Mine are wide open to all circling eyes,
filling up with eggs laid by the lady fly
who clung to the upright of my window frame
all of this hot fake summer winter's day
while her man rode her glossy back
and her wings shimmered,
shimmered and shimmered.

~

Not for me to ask,
do you remember?

Nowhere to walk
back to, together.
Not love of that kind.

What I touch
still bears your scent.
Love of that kind.

~

Listening long enough
of course I'll find that you're only
my own dream made flesh,
that the solitude you breathe
is the one I've found
and we inhabit the same torn air,
separated by skin and oceans

each of us setting out
for the same impossible sky,
raising loneliness like a flag
on each memory we reach.

~

This is a happy story.

Couldn't be otherwise,
given your life
and mine, given
but not taken.

Happy.
A story.
Long ago.
Far away.

FOLK DANCING FOR BEGINNERS

He sets the tone

In my country the president
rises
from a bed of red carnations

and then the children
sit down
each with a goldfish on their desk.

Their task is to teach it to
swim
better than it does already.

At the end of the year they'll
have to have to have to
show what it can do

and the president will
visit
with gifts of sandwiches and white flags.

So where were you

when I needed you?

I know, you were right here,
staring at me from the doorstep
saying get a grip, your needs are a joke

and of course you were right,
they were, I did.

Now you've come all the way in
and you're turning this way and that
in front of the mirror, offering me

a whole wardrobe of postures to record
breathlessly, and I'm trying not to yawn.

Show me something that makes me
want to dress up to match,
show me the germ of a good time, show me
something silkier than I can spin myself

and I'm all yours,
me and my fine adjectives,
all yours.

The laws of physics are inviolable

Now I realise
I just assumed
you'd be willing to share my lunch,
lend me your books, borrow mine.

Now I realise
you'd look at me and think
'you're of no interest'.

You'd never need a lift from me,
I'd never dream of asking you for one.

Parallel phone lines stretched
pole to pole along the national road.
Or an underpass and a flyover.
Both unending, and if I can look at you so nakedly
it's because not even my shadow exists in your world.
It's a plastic bag blown against a fence,
you pass it with your shades on, turning the volume up.

I wish I could tease you and pour you a drink,
I wish you'd laugh sometimes
and wonder what I'm thinking.

I can't keep scowling, it's bad for my heart
yet that's the only way I can stop you
flattening me with your clown-size mirror,
your nothing there but policy documents
bursting out of your pockets,
your voice like a jumbo all-the-trimmings hot dog.

Take your places

A scarf is the opposite of a piece of ground
and what is the opposite of a nickel blade?

A street corner is the opposite of a nectarine.
Where do a trestle table and a hundred lemons meet?

To skip takes a certain history of bare toes.
There are no reflections in a lift shaft.

Where fingertips have married marble
centuries have passed in a blaze of silk

and all the wooden residue turns to amethyst
whispering gold-veined secrets as the lights go out.

Where to from here?

You learn a lot of tricks along the way
that don't seem like tricks at the time
until you realise you're doing them in your sleep,
all those heartfelt gestures and complex rhythms.

I've been reading prophecies written thirty years ago
that tell exactly how the grand betrayal would happen
twenty years later, and I think about the man who wrote them
sitting in a malaria-infested camp in a foreign country,
hidden guest of sympathetic enemies,
thinking about how he could defend himself
against his dangerous comrades when they summoned him
to account for his claims that they were running
                              businesses with donor funds,
running legs of lamb with gun money begged from
                                        starving supporters,
setting up bursary funds for their own children with the
                                        soldiers' shoe allowance,
thinking about how he would have to pretend to like
                              legs of lamb and briefcases
to get out of there alive.

Where to from here?
He died as soon as he got out.
Let's sit still a while and watch
earthworms explaining things to eggshells.

The coastline seems endless

Everyone returns after a while.

The one you loved comes back
as a YouTube clip and you understand
why he left without you,

the one who loved you
comes back as the president
of a club your parents joined
at the time you ran away,

the one you were
wakes up one night
inside you

begging for mercy
in a voice you hoped
never to hear again.

But here they all are,
none of them looking at you
and all you can do is wait
for them to find you
ghosting their nights and days
and reach out, ready to try again.

It goes like this

First come the loud boys leaping sideways
thinner than my heart.

The girls say come, come, come
and the boys leap, and the wind blows,
its small kitten paws smacking the day
slightly skew and rosy.

They are throwing their arms around you.
Oh! how warm they feel!
They are throwing their arms around you.
Oh! be careful!

                ~

The men in dark suits cross the stage in formation.
They are very tired.
They will have a drink standing up.
They will head for their cars without seeming to hurry.
There are hairbrushes somewhere, waiting for them.

                ~

At the entrance to the country
the women beat drums
outside their front doors. They are so angry, their jerseys
stretch and snap in the wind.
Then they go inside without a word.

                ~

Oh sad and skinny boys I can't get past you,
you're like fence staves across my road,
knobbly branches broken off and made to stand sentry
without a crossbar or knitted arteries of wire
to hold you steady, your bony smiles reassure no one.

You have ten ways to stave off hunger,
none of them good, and if I tried to hug you
you'd be shy and brutal in response, awkwardly
you'd stab me and run, and rightly so,
you have a gift for leaping through alleys to find shelter
from the wind that scours the last flesh
from your dreams, the wind in eyes like mine,
you fuck and smoke and sleep the hours into a brave
history around the thinness of your heart,
its eager smile, you know you could do something,
if it were only possible.

You are here

A bin
a concrete table
half a pigeon wing
a eucalyptus tree.

Standing at the edge of the gravel
I look into a valley.
It floats and folds like the cloak of a story.

Words wander through it
harvesting the air – rustling ants, furrowing worms,
just, just audible.

     ~

I put in petrol,
get the windscreen cleaned, give R5.

You overtake me wildly,
I hug the yellow safety lane.

Thank you, your hazards flash
and my brights flash, you're welcome.

     ~

Only here, only here
in an enormous country
love is a small and private thing
running freely between cars, across valleys,
up and down the Shoprite aisles
finding its missing parts in the wire bins
with the Special Offer crowns.

Balancing

How much does it weigh,
this ribbon of hours slipping into the sunburnt sea?

grains of air, splinters of blue water —

The woman in the orange skirt — her hands like flying fish
laughing as they splash the sea over her hot shoulders,
how much, how little do they weigh?

we try to balance them, but how — on our own hands? on the light?

And the toddler's screams of upside-down rage in his sister's arms
to be put down, set free to wriggle into the jewel bed of shells,
do they weigh more than the mine shaft his father's father dug?

— or count them, but it's like counting your own breaths,
you get lost in the breathing of them, each one is the first —

How much does the beach weigh,
relative to the hectare of houses queuing at one old standpipe?
How light is this single day spread out on a striped towel,
relative to three centuries flooded with loss?

Between and between, the taxi van stands with its doors open,
its dusty mats glittering with the salt prints of feet
clambering in to fetch a sunhat, jumping out again.

— and this is where we've got to, and this is where we are for now

Acknowledgements and Notes

p. 1   *'Photographing the building is forbidden until the war is over'*
Sign outside the US Consulate, Cape Town, c. 2004

p. 12   *Specialised*
'Ammunition Airlift During the Relief of Khe Sanh, South Vietnam,
April, 1968': a colour photograph by Larry Burrows (originally part of a
Life photo essay, on exhibition in New York, reprinted in *The New Yorker*).

p. 14   *Skypointing*
'skypointing', 'appeasement', 'gannets' and 'coastal colonies' – words on a
public education poster prepared by the Department of Trade and
Industry.

p. 20   *Monument to the South African Republic (On some photographs by
David Goldblatt)*
The photographs by David Goldblatt to which the poem refers are:
'Memorials to two policemen shot and killed here by robbers on 3 July
2002, Whipp Street, Memel, Free State. Three men were each given two
life sentences for the murders, 24 August 2005.'
'Monument to the Republic of South Africa 31 May 1961, Cornelia, Free
State, 24 August 2005.'
'Memorial to two members of the African armed forces killed in what
President PW Botha called the "Total Onslaught", Villiers, Free State, 24
August 2005.'

p. 34   *In the empty station*
'birds fly through the empty station': a line that could be Tom Raworth's,
could belong to the Tom I knew for one evening in London in 1978.

p. 40   *Thank you Lee Smolin, thank you Mr Leibniz*
Lee Smolin's book *The Life of the Cosmos* (Phoenix, 1997) is gratefully
acknowledged.

p. 95   *Three meditations on Why is there war, Mummy?*
'Against the hyper-legibility of the violent act' is quoted from André
Lepecki and Jenn Joy (eds), *Planes of Composition. Dance, Theory, and the
Global* (Seagull Books, 2009), p. XV.

p. 115   *Tango for person and city*
abrazo: embrace; *salida*: exit (a pattern that begins a figure); *amagues*: threats,

feints; *volcadas*: extreme leans; *baldoso*: 'tile' (a six-step figure); *caricias*: caresses; *caminando*: walking; *golpecitos*: little toe taps between steps; *cadencias*: stepping in place, marking time; *molinete*: 'windmill' (walking in a wheel around the hub, i.e. the leader); *cruzada*: a 'chase' with a 'cross' (one way to go from the outside to the inside position); *resolución*: resolution. Thank you, Wikipedia.

p. 127   *Phendukani Silwani*
Nobuntu Mazeka is gratefully acknowledged for her detailed account of the conditions of Phendukani Silwani's life and death, which provided the source material for this poem.